A Message to Black College Students

By: JerJuan Howard

JerJuan A. Howard Books/ Plug'd Media LLC. 2020

ISBN: 978-0-9960943-8-2

Published in Detroit, Michigan.

What others are saying about "A Message to Black College Students

"I've read this masterpiece and it's tool that goes beyond the black college student. Particularly the "False Perception of Success...."- Dr. Kenneth Howard (Author and Professor at Wayne State University)

"Fire. Engaging, easy to follow, and makes the point quickly with the 20 pages." - Kyle McMurtry (Howard University Student & Author of Henry goes to a HBCU)

"A very clear message. A concerning address to the Black college student." - Joelle Sanders (Junior at Western Michigan University, Sports Management Major)

A Message to Black College Students

"This book holds great significance to the Black community as it promotes accountability and self-sufficiency." - Alona Turner (Clark Atlanta University Alumni, Marketing Major)

"Encourages conversation, education, growth, and action. Great read!" - Arnitra Randolph (Sophomore at Eastern Michigan University, General Business Major)

"A book that should be read by all past, current, and future Black college students." - Warren Richardson (Senior at Western Michigan University, Physics Major)

Dedication

I dedicate this book to my late mother Jerwana. The hours that you spent praying for me surely have paid off and I want to acknowledge the role that your faith has played in my life. Thank you for making my life a priority.

I dedicate this book to my late grandparents Virginia and Tommy Davis. They taught me, at a young age, the importance of "it takes a village". You both installed confidence into me and made me believe that I could do anything I put my mind to. This book would not be possible without the life values and lessons that you provided me with.

I dedicate this book to my mentor/brother Khalil Masi-Hill. The first person to truly recognize me as a leader and problem solver during my

collegiate studies. You've invested a lot of time into me. A true intellectual and a leader that I respect.
I dedicate this book to Walter Malone. My first black instructor at Western Michigan University. A man that changed my view of what it meant to be a black college student.
I dedicate this book to the Black Student Union of Western Michigan University. This organization taught me the importance of being around like-minded individuals. We all have power as individuals but as a collective, we are much stronger.

Table of Contents

Introduction

A Message to Black College Students was written to serve as a wake-up call to Black college students of the past, present, and future. I hope it serves as a resource for Black students as they navigate through their college experience and beyond. My plan for this book is to provide a new understanding that may shift the mindset of those who read it. View this book as a tool for the entire Black community to unify, organize, and serve as a catalyst for collective Black progression. Allow it to serve as a key to unlocking the endless potential that I know we all have. It should be noted that I'm a Black college student myself; therefore, I'm holding Black college students accountable because I've seen firsthand what we can do once given the right tools.

When faced with a problem in our community, we have two obligations—which should be broken down by the amount of time, energy, and resources we put into each one. We have an obligation to do for self and to hold authority accountable. Holding authority accountable only gets us so far. The real progression comes from us. We must develop a "do for self" mindset and become our own saviors by being less dependent on outside activity and more dependent on our own community strength to solve our problems. For instance, if we have a problem with bad representation in media, we should create our own media outlets to represent us holistically. Tyler Perry did this by taking matters into his own hands instead of pleading with networks to properly represent the Black community.

There is a sociocultural war going on, and this war is against Black people in the justice system, Black health, Black economics, and definitely Black intellectualism. Black college students must realize their role in this war by first acknowledging that there is an actual war happening. Secondly, we must recognize that we are being used as pawns for the opposing side's army. We are unknowingly supporting the Eurocentric systems and individualistic ideas that help oppress our people...the *opposite* of our progression.

War is strategic and intentional. Every move and decision has a deeper purpose. In turn, we have to be just as strategic and deliberate with our influence and decision making. Not all wars are physical fights with guns and bombs. I believe that the most important ones are mental. War on perception. War on value systems. War on information. War on priorities. War on real history. Once the mind is conquered, the body follows. Once the body is conquered, the day-to-day actions of those conquered will reflect the interests of whatever conquered them in the first place. The influence may be a person, a system, etc.

I'm conflicted as I write this book. I don't want non-Black people (outsiders) who read

A Message to Black College Students to view Black college students as discombobulated. Nevertheless, the first step to progression is reflection. Therefore, I hold the Black college student to a standard that is higher than any person, place, or system opposing them. Collectively, we will figure this out. I urge you to read this book in its entirety, in order, to fully understand my message.

-J. Howard

Stop Trying to Separate Yourself from Other Black People

Stop doing everything in your power to separate from the masses of other Black people. If you must separate yourself temporarily to "level up", make sure it is with the mindset of reconnecting and bringing back what you've learned to make the masses better. By separating, some of us are supporting the same system that we claim to oppose.

Don't become someone who continuously tries to separate themselves from other Black people in disguise of "bettering themselves." Direct opposition to Eurocentric obedience is Black unity. Eurocentric obedience involves greedy capitalism, individualism, and forgetting our ancestors' fight, to name a few. Greedy capitalism involves making an idol of currency, placing it above unity, progression, and the holistic well-being of Black people.

Individualism is directly linked to greedy capitalism. It is the belief that individual success outweighs collective advancement. These are concepts that fuel white supremacy. Therefore, Black obedience to those concepts is an ally of white supremacy. If you imitate a people, you are those people.

"No one is self-made, especially Black people." This simple statement is extremely important, as it allows you to better understand our people. I recommend observing people to see what they represent. Don't judge, observe. Are their actions rooted in individualism or collectivism? Please pay close attention to the value system of any Black person who only looks out for himself or herself and feels no connection to the struggles of those who have come before them. Do the organizations that they are a part of cause unnecessary separation? Does their neighborhood cause unnecessary separation? These are questions we must ask. This separation that I speak of can come in two different forms: mental separation or physical separation.

Physical separation is a little easier to undo than mental separation. An example of physical separation is moving away from other Black people to the suburbs or going off to college and never looking back. People who want to be physically separated say things like, "Detroit is ghetto. I prefer Auburn Hills." It's the ideology that "white ice is colder." Mental separation, on the other hand, requires more effort when attempting to re-develop a mindset of advancing the collective.

Oftentimes, the Black college student becomes so mentally exhausted in this constant uphill battle that they separate themselves from Black thoughts and Black struggles. Instead of being their genuine selves, it's easier for them to land an internship while masking as something or someone they aren't. In their mind, the goal of collective Black progression is out the window. They look out for themselves or very few people close to them. They say things like, "Well...I made it out, so can they," "They aren't working hard enough," and "That's not my business...I can only help me." These are tell-tale signs of a mentally separated Black college student. They are isolated in their way of thinking, and they've become shallow and cold to the struggles of those who share numerous commonalities with them. This, unfortunately, is the mindset that a lot of Black people carry. We praise Italian clothing brands but ask for discounts with Black-owned brands. We prefer to study Greek philosophy over African scholars. We commend the general student government organizations and give little to no credit to the Black student organizers on campus. We've been brainwashed to support and love everything that isn't a direct representation of us. Black college students have to wake up. We have to realize how powerful, influential, and intelligent we can be for our people.

Part of the reason we separate mentally is because we allow outside judgment to tell us what our communities are worth. Our systems and cultures aren't tailored to succeed in the environments of others. This is why the Black community is in the condition that it's in. We expect to have individualistic ideals and a progressive Black community. That isn't our culture. It's never been, and it never will be. **If you judge a fish by how fast it can run down the street, then you'll have a struggling fish. If you judge a Black community by how well they can adjust to an individualistic and cut-throat society, then you'll have a struggling Black community.** The fish does not grow legs in an effort to run down the street. Instead, the fish is doing everything possible to return back to water. Instead of the Black community trying to squeeze our way into a society through efforts that cause moral degradation, we should focus on building our own society that has our values ingrained into it. Individualism isn't our way of life, and it shows the more we try to fit into these standards and systems. We are tribal people who care about one another.

In addition, part of this mental separation is attributed to the media that we consume. We cast a harsh judgment on Black communities based on biased news reports that ignore the underlying issues that have caused certain areas to have unfavorable conditions. For instance, a popular news outlet routinely highlights gang activity while simultaneously ignoring the lack of educational resources within this community. A lack of resources has led many community members to partake in unorthodox behaviors: drug distribution/consumption, theft, physical altercations, etc. Picture being a young Black boy in an impoverished community, watching these news outlets portray members within your community, friends even, as violent thugs that perpetuate heinous crimes. Naturally, this young boy will begin to fetishize other communities. His goal will no longer be to better his community, instead his new aim is to flee from it. In this instance, the media has managed to control the narrative of this neighborhood and the citizens within it. Our minds are delicate, as such, they can be easily tainted. It is important that we do not allow these biased news reports to control the narrative of our people. If you continuously digest rhetoric that alludes to our communities being dangerous and unruly, for no acceptable reason, then the media has fulfilled its part in our mental separation. Essentially, these reports have given the Black community member just cause to mentally isolate themselves from their community. It's shallow for any person to make claims about our communities being slums without looking at the events that got us to that point.

Let's take a moment and talk about outsourcing and how it has led to our communities becoming slums and ghettos with which no one wants to be involved. **Outsourcing** is when a person is a part of a community, but they go outside of that community for necessary or desired goods or services. Imagine if a community had businesses, schools, and grocery stores inside of it. Now imagine the people in the community spending their money at businesses on the other side of town, sending their children to schools 30 minutes away from their home, and driving across town for groceries. What do you expect to happen to that community? It is destined to become an impoverished area. Outsourcing has played a part in destroying the economic foundation of many Black communities. Once the community is driven to this state, physical and mental separation is easy.

Our False Perception of Success has Hindered the Black Community

Black people's perceptions and ideas of success can no longer be the same as America's perception of success. **As long as the Black college student continues to view personal achievement as the only type of success, the Black community as a whole will always lack.**

Personal achievements such as big homes, new cars, and positions in big corporations (e.g., Wall Street, Apple, Google, etc.) can no longer be used as measuring sticks on how successful a recent Black graduate is. None of these things help the community collectively.

We must learn to celebrate our own to create opportunities for us. For example, the Black law student shouldn't have to worry about competition from white law students for a job in a corporate law firm. Once he or she graduates, there should be systems in place allowing the Black law student to be hired at a Black law firm: a firm that represents the

Black community's interests. If no law firm is tailored toward the skills and values of the individual and community at large, then the Black law student should be focused on creating his or her own law firm with like-minded individuals. Taking this route will allow Black law students to do two things. Firstly, they will control the entire board instead of being a pawn in someone else's game. Secondly, they become a direct resource to the Black community. Building these structures empowers us all.

Building by no means is an easy feat. It is much easier to join big corporations, go on about everyday life, and never reach a hand back to help the community that needs you more than anything else. That's what so many Black college students and graduates are doing today. It's much more difficult for 25 Black students and 25 community members to come together and get a plan of action going—a plan that will have long-lasting positive change within the community. The community members have always had open arms when it comes to these collaborations. It's the Black college student that must take this step toward progression.

How We Got To This Point

In *The Souls of Black Folk*, W.E.B Du Bois talked about double consciousness, the idea of having several identities at the same time. Double consciousness is the feeling that your identity is divided into several parts, making it difficult or impossible to have one particular identity. I see a constant battle of double consciousness—the identity of being American and Black at the same time—within the lives of Black college students.

It's tough balancing these two identities because they carry two different sets of ideals and morals. American ideology believes that you must achieve the "American dream" at all costs. Black ideology tells us to leave no one behind and to be generous to those that lack. American ideology teaches us that there is pride in being "self-made" and that you must "pay to play." Black ideology teaches us to take pride in the idea that "it takes a village..." and the greatest investment you can make is to invest in someone's mind; thus, we take pride in teaching one another. The return on investment on the American home-front differs from the return on investment on the Black home-front.

This non-stop battle has helped land Black people in the predicament that we are in now. We have to choose who we are going to be in an unapologetic fashion. We have to decide which identity's ideals and morals we will follow—American or Black. One identity will undoubtedly outweigh the other, but I believe that there can be a balance. I cannot tell you what your specific balance will be, but I do have some suggestions.

Surviving in America means that certain American ideals must be followed. For example, American currency is used to buy clothes, food, products, and so on. If you need a specific product or service from another person, then the American dollar doesn't necessarily have to be your sole choice of currency. If you're good at editing resumes and someone else is good at editing college papers, then you can use your skills as currency, instead of money. This said, we can barter within our community and weaken our dependence on American ideals, such as the dollar bill.

No one's self-made. Black people who view themselves as self-made are usually less likely to help others; therefore, taking away from the "it takes a village" ideology. Our culture's contemporary obsession with being *self-made* is dangerous. Any successful person has had help along the way, whether they admit it or not. That help may have come from a book, moral support, inspiration, community member, mentor, past leader and so on. In any case, someone or something aided in your success, at some point. All assistance isn't monetary. Currently, we operate within the mindset that anyone who has had to overcome poverty, with little to no monetary assistance, is self-made. This mindset is extremely dangerous for two specific reasons.

Firstly, it requires assimilation into the American ideal that enforces money as the ultimate end goal. As Black people, we do not have the luxury of personal financial stability being our only end. We must push past this mile marker, in order to cultivate a more progressive society for future generations. To effectively make lasting change, we must invest in our neighborhoods, when possible, reach back, when applicable, and provide inspiration. Imagine what the current state of Black people would be if our ancestors adopted this same mindset. Certainly, they received very little, if any, handouts. However, they were still consumed with the mindset "it takes a village." They cultivated a tribe so strong that they were able to overcome adversities, as well as, pave the way for future generations of Black people. We are charged with this same responsibility to achieve beyond personal monetary gain and to cultivate a village that makes it possible for you, and those around you to overcome all adversaries our people face.

Secondly, We've built our identities on dysfunction. We honor those who are self-made and struggle throughout their life, but look down on people who've had decent upbringings and label them *silver spoon*. Ideologies like these directly oppose our progression. I understand that some had it harder than others. However, there are deep psychological issues with being "self-made," and these issues play a part in our community's stance as a whole. We have been plagued with the stereotypes of being lazy and looking for hand-outs. The irony of this is that the ones who label us these things are the grand recipients of hand-outs. The same ones who tell us to pull ourselves up by our bootstraps are the same descendants of those who stole our entire boots to begin with.

Due to these stereotypes, we want no connection with assistance even though we are the ones who deserve it the most. We distance ourselves from collective help and collective work. I challenge you to be intentional about who you help. Let's get back to our ideals so that Black boys and girls in the future no longer have to carry the burden of being self-made. Like the African proverb says, "**Many hands make light work**." The society around us has taught us to value certain things over others. If a behavior is learned then it can also be unlearned.

Throughout *A Message to Black College Students,* I place the burden of progression on our shoulders, but it is not my intent to do so without acknowledging the part that America has played in our current socioeconomic status. At my university and many others across the country, Black college students are not succeeding academically at a rate that we could. Black college students are plagued with poor graduation and persistence rates in comparison to other races.

According to the U.S. Department of Education, National Center for Education Statistics, Integrated Postsecondary Education Data System (IPEDS), Winter 2016–17, first-time, full-time undergraduate Black college students have the lowest 4-year graduation rate (21%). Asian college students have the highest 4-year graduation rate (50%), followed by white college students (45%), with an overall average of all races at 41%. In terms of 6-year graduation rates for first time, full-time students, Black undergraduate students have an average of 40% which is second to last behind American Indian/Alaska Native (39%). The highest 6-year graduation rate for first-time, full-time undergraduate students was Asian students

(74%), followed by white students (64%), students of Two or more races (60%), Hispanic students (54 %), and an overall average of 60%.

According to the National Student Clearinghouse Research Center, in Fall 2017, Black college students had the lowest persistence rate of all races (66.2%), just over half of black students returned to the starting institution (52.1%) and an additional 14.1% continued at a different institution. Asian students had the highest persistence rate (84.7%), followed by white students (78.1%), and an overall average of 73.8% for all races.

Graduation & Persistence Rates by Race
Scan (QR Code for Graphs & Data)

These poor rates are not by coincidence. They are due to the faulty programs at these universities that have been used to pump Black students for their dollars before dumping them. The less than desirable graduation and retention rates of the Black college student are a result of four categories: economic, social, academic, and student involvement. These four categories are the determining factors as to whether or not Black college students will thrive or fail at universities. While student involvement falls directly on the shoulders of Black students, universities have failed in the other three areas. The university can offer a variety of programs and organizations to the student, but it cannot make a student get involved. Yes, the university could broadcast and advertise these programs more, but it is the responsibility of the Black college student to actually be involved. This is a microcosm of the lives in the Black community. While community involvement falls solely on Black citizens, America has also failed the Black citizen economically, socially, and academically.

If the Black college student is economically sound, then he or she can afford to stay in school and finish their studies. There are usually scholarships in place or university resources to help the college student since the university was responsible for the recruiting of that student in the first place. In the event that the Black college student is unaware of his or her resources, then the university—in turn—has failed the Black college student economically. As aforementioned, the same concept applies for the Black citizen. If he or she is unaware of the economic programs, business grants, etc. they are entitled to, then America's systems have failed them.

The second category that affects the Black college student's graduation and retention rates involve the social aspect of college life. According to testimonies from the students at my university, students stay where they feel welcomed and included. Retention rates are directly linked to student engagement activity. Knowingly, if Black students feel welcomed and included in their collegiate years, then they are more likely to stay enrolled in their universities. If they do not feel welcomed and/or included on campus, then they often isolate themselves, which usually leads to the dropping out of college. In many cases, this isolation is a result of the university's failure to acknowledge the students' interests, perspective, and history. If the university wanted to make Black college students feel welcomed, then they would make the comfort and inclusion of Black students a priority; however, universities intentionally do not. For example, currently at the vast majority of college institutions, African American studies are considered to be electives, courses not required by the university. However, if these universities truly sought to include black college students, these courses would be required curriculum, not just for black students but for each student seeking to attain higher education. Likewise, if America truly sought to include Black people into its society, then it would start in the school system. The inventions and advancements made by Black people in this country would be celebrated by everyone instead of hidden and isolated from the rest of history.

Despite a lack of acceptance, in nearly all aspects of society, Black people still have a history of making the best out of the worst. We have managed to cultivate innovative ways to find beauty in being "Outsiders". Our Art, Blues, and Hip Hop, are examples of creative solutions that form from societal isolation and a lack of inclusion.

Now, let's talk about academics. Similar to feeling included, if the Black college student is in good academic standing, then he or she usually withstands his or her collegiate years by graduating. If the Black college student is not academically sound, then he or she usually receives additional help from a tutor or respective professor. It is noticed that we learn better from those we can relate to, there aren't many people we can relate to and get help from in most of the universities in the country, unfortunately. Once students are no longer academically sound, they drop out of college, thus lowering the graduation and retention rates for Black college students even more.

Academia is a crucial part of life. When the educational system drives off the Black student—who is also the Black citizen—with irrelevant classes, distorted history, and non-correlating life subject areas, it may taint his or her interest in academia. For instance, when I could not find the relevance in the curriculum while in school, I would lose motivation. I viewed the assignments as nothing more than a grade and completed my coursework without enthusiasm or effort. This is an example of America failing the Black citizen by failing the Black student. This failure narrows down education to subject areas that aren't tailored to Black life or Black culture. This is not a coincidence.

If the Black college student manages to conquer the four categories that likely hinder graduation, then he or she has a better chance of earning his or her degree. The only problem is that, according to the data, only a very small percentage of Black college students make it to this point. Seeing your peers slowly dropout of college can have a lingering effect on your mind.

Those who manage to handle the economic, social, and academic disparities while maintaining school involvement usually don't see the systemic issues with college and the role it plays in the lives of students who didn't finish. The same goes for Black citizens who make it out of their neighborhoods. They may not see the systemic issues because they were not directly impacted by them and therefore don't have an urge to help fix them.

I give these examples to show that our issues are deeply rooted, intentional, and systemic. **Although we, Black people, are not completely responsible for our current state in the world, we are responsible for our advancement.**

The Wrong Definition of Black Excellence

It is not enough for us to honor a Black person solely because of their sophisticated title. One becomes honorable once he or she uses the credentials or title(s) that they have for the advancement of Black academics, Black economics, Black health, and Black culture. **It doesn't matter how successful a Black doctor is if the community cannot afford his or her services.**

We can no longer honor a Black politician just because they're Black. A politician has power in spaces that others do not; and until that politician uses that power for the advancement of other Black people, the politician isn't honorable.

We can no longer honor a successful entrepreneur just because they're Black. The Black entrepreneur who has accumulated massive wealth is not necessarily honorable solely because of his or her wealth. That entrepreneur has power in spaces (i.e., knowledge, money) that the rest of us do not;

and if this power isn't being used in ways that can help others, then the entrepreneur isn't honorable.

No Black organization should be considered prestigious unless they are doing prestige work to uplift the masses of Black people. We can no longer honor any person, place, or idea that isn't directly attached to enhancing the Black community. The younger generations want to be viewed as honorable, so they repeat these ideals, pushing us further from the goal of collective progression.

The mis-leadership class of Black people grows larger and stronger with people in positions of power who look like us but are not using their positions to benefit us. This is the vicious cycle we face. Far too often, we get tricked into believing that everyone Black with some success under their belt stands for Black progression when their everyday actions and choices tell us otherwise. This is false, and it's a belief that must quickly change. I'm not here to bash our brothers and sisters, but take a look around you. Look at the Black people in positions of power and ask yourself two questions.

The first question is, "Is this person teaching collective self-sufficiency and empowerment?" If they aren't teaching or practicing these things, then they're in no position to be leaders for Black progression. Whatever is not empowering you is more than likely draining you. Anyone not practicing the "do for self" mentality is putting you and other Black people in situations to be dependent on something else besides our community. Historically, this has never been good for us. We slip into a powerless state with no real leveraging power to get the things we need for our families and communities. This position leaves us dependent on outside sources such as self-serving government officials, faulty assistance systems, and people who don't have our best interest at heart. For example, let's say our people don't own the local grocery store in our community, and that grocery store decides that it doesn't want to sell produce anymore. How will you and your community eat? What systems does the community have in place to feed each other? We cannot solely depend on voting to be the only source of power. We have to have separate systems and gain an understanding among ourselves as well. Voting isn't going to stop the fact that we have no real bargaining power when it comes to external affairs within our communities. We have to organize and build these systems for our own.

The second question is, "Does this person address the root causes of our problems or just the symptoms?" Many leaders today tend to focus on the symptoms of the problem and turn a blind eye to the real root causes. For example, if a person is hungry, then he or she may decide to commit crimes in order to get money for food. Crime, in this case, would be a symptom of the root cause: poverty. In a similar scenario, if a person is hungry, then he or she may decide to go to the local food pantry to get just enough food to feed themselves for a few days. This "alternative" to the original example does not truly change the hungry person's situation because the root cause is poverty, not hunger. Until that person has the knowledge and resources to grow his or her own food, the problem will remain.

We've continued to focus our attention on ways to combat crime and start new assistance programs. However, these attempts have offered no long-term solutions. The reason being, these short-term solutions continuously ignore the root cause of issues. Instead, these resources attack the symptoms. I am in no way stating that charities and other services have no role in progression. However, it is important that we understand the difference between corporate-led assistance programs and community-ran service initiatives. Corporate-led assistance programs seek to exploit those in need for tax write-offs and merit. Conversely, community-ran service initiatives seek to better the lives of its members while simultaneously uplifting all parties involved.

The Black community has been put last for decades. No one is going to save us but us. Black college students must graduate, get their degree-skill, and then go back into the community to take a step toward using that skill to advance our people. This is the real definition of Black Excellence.

For instance, I'm sure the Black mechanical engineering major can learn from the local Black mechanic that has had his business for ten years. And vice versa, the local Black mechanic can learn about new and current systems of engineering vehicles from the recent mechanical engineering graduate. How about the local gardening organizations such as D-Town Farms, MyHopeVillage, and PeaceTree Park? These organizations have qualities (e.g., knowledge about diet and herbs, a sense of community, overall wellness, etc.)

that a Black nutrition major would find useful. The local gardener, in turn, can surely benefit from the experience of the nutrition major. Community organizers—such as New Era Detroit—know public policies and how they directly impact our communities...knowledge that a Black political science major would find valuable in his or her fight to transform our communities.

The type of collaboration mentioned above is crucial to the advancement of the Black community; nonetheless, it won't come to fruition until both sides see that it is necessary. Both parties must be willing to come together in a shared space and collaborate on ideas. Black college students must step down from our pedestal and go into these opportunities with an open and collaborative mindset. We have endless potential once we decide to humble ourselves and unify. Be sure to reach back and use your skill with your people every chance that you get.

It is important to not always attach money to the idea of giving back. Some of the most significant forms of giving back have nothing to do with money. I still remember the names of every teacher that helped me believe I was smart and instilled confidence in me at a very young age. Without the knowledge poured into me by James Howard, Walter Malone, Khalil Masi, Raphael Wright, Jewell Jones, Malik Yakini, and many more, this book would not exist. I am who I am because of who we all are. Likewise, as a Black college student, you have the power to be that inspiration for someone else. This is the tribe and sense of community that we have to expand on.

Dear Black elitists, please go away! The superiority complex that Black college students carry must be addressed. We've allowed classism to get in the way of our connecting and pushing forward on a common goal. Are you loyal to your people or your socioeconomic class? Often, we as Black college students, carry a sense of superiority that blinds us from our commonalities with working-class Black people. **Do not confuse Black Elitism with Black Excellence.**

When faced with a problem, we have two obligations—which should be broken down by how much time, energy, and resources we put into each one. The first obligation we have when faced with a problem is to "do for self." This mentality should take up about 80% of your attention. The second obligation is "holding authority accountable," which should receive no more than 20% of your attention.

By now, we understand specific systems and how they oppress us. We know the way that they work. The more power we give them to feed us, the more power they have to starve us. The systems in place only have as much power as we provide them. Stop giving them the power to fix our problems. Holding the government accountable without doing anything for ourselves doesn't work.

Condemn them for the wrong that they've done but asking a contributor to be the solution to the problem is insane.

Our Communities> Corporate America

Our communities need you far more than corporate America does. You'll be more valuable using your skills with us than with them. Having complete control of the decisions being made on behalf of your profession is more important than working for a corporate agency. Having control of your own table is far more effective and powerful than barely having a seat at someone else's, regardless of the size of their table.

For those who are not familiar, I want to introduce you to the school-to-prison pipeline where the K-12 school system has structures similar or parallel to prison rules. For example, the zero tolerance policies and punishments that schools have in place, are similar to the zero tolerance policies and punishments that prisons have in place. Students are often instructed to walk in a straight line on the right side of the halls just as they are in prison. Teachers have authority over 20+ students, similar to the ratio between guards and inmates in prison. Along with the school-to-prison pipeline is a similar theory called the college-to-Corporate America pipeline. Just as a K-12 school can prepare a child for prison, college can prepare the Black student for Corporate America. Many college career fairs confirm this theory. College conforms students and strips us of most of our individuality, thus molding us into obedient workers in Corporate America.

In college, there are hard deadlines with your professor, parallel to Corporate America's rules with your boss. College students stay up all night to make sure a project is complete, similar to the work ethic of many Corporate America workers. **College has been used as a tunnel where Black students have entered through one side as creative, optimistic, and enthusiastic learners and have exited as graduates**

ready to become a part of the workforce, instead of the driving force for Black communities. This is why it is crucial to "play the game" to change the game instead of getting submerged in it. When submerging happens, we conform to what education and success is by someone else's standards—which is designed to prepare us for a career that will make someone else wealthy. We conform to what intelligence is based on a small checklist. As a result, we are blind to what real knowledge is. If one of our own doesn't conform to these intelligence standards, then they'll have limited alternative options to broadcast their intelligence. The late rapper Nipsey Hussle described it like this: "He knows he's a genius. He just can't claim it because they left him no platforms to explain it." It is up to you to make that platform to broadcast your intelligence and the intelligence of your people.
According to the NATIONAL

POSTSECONDARY STUDENT AID SURVEY: 2015-2016, the U.S. DEPARTMENT OF EDUCATION discovered that a Black student who has earned a Bachelor's degree has an average of $4,274 more in student loan debt than his or her white peer. The student loan system in America requires college students to start paying off debt six months after graduation. This means some form of income is needed immediately after earning a degree

Student Loan Debt By Race
Scan QR Code for Graphs & Data

Knowingly, if the Black college student takes on a job from a corporate agency, then he or she should have the mindset of playing the game to change the game. In other words, Black college students should use the money, knowledge, and experience in Corporate America to build their careers with their people. Far too often, we settle for jobs where we're undervalued.

Think of internships and how they're distributed. Many of us understand how tough it can be for a Black college student to land a paid internship. How great would it be for you to give a Black college student an internship at your company and/or organization? Once again, no one is going to save us but us. Once we make it to a certain level, we must create opportunities for other Black people. That's how we build. This is the tribe!

Imagine working for a corporation that doesn't see a need in addressing the issues you see in your community. Imagine working for a law firm that knows the law and how to hold police accountable, but they don't. Imagine working for an engineering company with the knowledge and tools to help improve the structure of your neighborhood, but they choose not to. Imagine working for a corporation with the tools necessary to educate your community on finances, but the company decides not to. What voice do you have in these instances when you're a part of Corporate America? The answer is often little to none. The value, intelligence, and understanding you bring to the table is sometimes not appreciated. You're often replaceable. On the contrary, in an organization owned and controlled by the Black community, you're priceless!

You can use your skills to help the Black community without having to answer to anyone else. In doing so, the private interests of outside agencies will no longer control your creativity and desire to push for Black progression. Never underestimate the power you have as an individual and how much more powerful you'll become as a unit. **Networking horizontally has just as much power as networking vertically.** You and your peers have the brainpower to collectively cultivate an idea that can shift the world, but that idea will never come to fruition if you all are putting all of your energy into getting hired at a bigger company.

Everyone does not want to run a business and that is perfectly fine. In the instance that you do not want to own your own business then you should look to your people for employment. Aaliyah Gross explained it perfectly when she said: "If you have no desire to open your own law firm but have a law degree, then don't immediately look to

Corporate America for employment. Find a law firm owned by a like-minded individual in your community and help operate it. Use your skills to improve your community in whatever capacity you see fit, whether that's as an owner or employee. Both roles are essential. It's just as crucial for a Black college-educated entrepreneur to open a business that helps better serve his or her community as it is for a Black college-educated worker to seek employment within his or her community. Stop looking for jobs with others just because it's convenient. Instead, shift the norm of who controls employment within your community."

More times than not, Black progression is heavily based on entrepreneurship. While entrepreneurship is important, we leave out the people who want to be employees—not owners—when we solely focus on this business type.

Black college students aren't the saviors of the Black community, nor are we above the rest of the community. We aren't always the leaders of the community. We are a part of the community. We have a skill set that can benefit everyone, so we should use it as such.

What Are the Right Tools?

In the introduction of this book, I shared my observation on Black college students' capabilities once given the right tools. The right tools are a true knowledge of our history. **History is a weapon.**

Through a true knowledge of our history, we gain an understanding of our current state of affairs and its relationship to our future. We also gain inspiration and power from those who have come before us. There is no shortcut to this. We have to study the past in order to gain a better understanding of today. This type of understanding allows all of us to be on code moving forward. As we read and study history, we're empowered to connect the dots. History is more deep-rooted than Dr. Martin Luther King, Jr. and Malcolm X.

Who was Dr. Carter G. Woodson, and what was his theory? What was the topic in the debates between W.E.B Du Bois and Booker

T. Washington? What is Mound Bayou? What is the significance of Idlewild, Michigan? What was Camp Nizhoni, and how was it created? What is Pan-Africanism? What did Marcus Garvey think was key to Black liberation? What was Frederick Douglass' thought process, and what did he mean by "Power concedes nothing without a demand"? Who was Georgia Gilmore? What advancements did Elijah Muhammad and the Nation of Islam make for Black People? Who were Huey P. Newton and Bobby Seale, and what were their contributions to Black progression? Who is Angela Davis, and why is she important? Who was Audre Lorde, and why was she important? Could knowing Audre's ideas on intersectionality be useful for Black unity during this time? What is the philosophy of Rob Williams in terms of self-defense in the Black community? Why did W.E.B leave the NAACP? Who was Septima Clark, and what augmentations did she make? Who is Kwame Ture? Who is Toni

Morrison? What are Dr. Claud Anderson's ideas regarding the empowerment of the Black community?

The big question we all must know the answer to involves COINTELPRO. What is it? Which American organization created it? What effects did it have on Black progression movements in the past? What role did the media play in all of this? What tactics were used? What effect did COINTELPRO have on the Garvey Movement and the Black Panther Party? Specific tactics were used to infiltrate, disrupt, discredit, and divide our movements, such as: tarnishing the reputation of our leaders(cancel culture), creating division between Black men and Black women, and even betraying Black people with a promise for a better life. Are these same tactics being used today? It is on you—the reader—to study and find answers to the above mentioned questions. The Black mind needs the right tools to move forward, and you have the choice to equip yourself accordingly.

Gil Scott Heron said "The revolution will not be televised" and this is valid. The revolution has to take place in your mind before it takes place anywhere else. You must be the person who decides that what's happening can no longer be good enough for you, your community, or your people. The strength is in everyone being on code. The ideology that we need one leader is the reason why it has been hard for Black people to make progress from the 60s through the 70s. **We made the mistake of placing the burden of Black progression on the backs of leaders and not ourselves. Once those leaders were killed, people started to look for the next leader, when they should've looked in the mirror.** The great Fred Hampton said, "You can kill the revolutionary, but you can't kill the revolution." This is true. Once you make one person the entire revolution, it's easy to kill it. That's why "the revolution" is more effective in our minds.

A Message to Black College Students provides us with additional tools to fight this current battle for Black progression. There is much more history to cover than what is mentioned; nonetheless, this is a start. No single Black movement had all the right answers, but we must build off of the past mistakes instead of starting completely over and repeating the same ones. **If we can become students of our history, then we can take something from all our ancestors and use their experiences to help ours. We can learn their theories and put them into practice in our lives.**

Progress > Recognition

Black college students in 2020 seem to value recognition more than progress, which is a very dangerous ideology to have. Through observation, I've found that there are many Black organizations on college campuses that have similar mission statements and purposes but are fighting for the same general body members. This type of unnecessary competition does great harm to the Black community on any college campus, be it a Historically Black College and University (HBCU) or a Predominately White Institution (PWI). It hinders progress because it directly combats Black unity. The root cause of this problem is the fact that we value recognition more than we value development. **Our value system is skewed.**

In our current climate, titles and recognition appear to be more glamorous and prestigious than being a part of a more significant cause. Knowingly, some people have undercut others with hopes of getting to the next stage of recognition. We've come to value being recognized as a founder or president of an organization rather than simply coming together and pulling resources to be one loud, powerful voice. The demands of Black college students are more respected when we have one common agenda paired with an authoritative tone, advocating for one thing. Five or six different voices can dilute the message. It creates an image of being unorganized and, once again, decreases the likelihood of progress. That said, no real progress is going to come without unity. It will take the Black college student to look at himself or herself in the mirror and figure out what's important in uplifting every Black person. We either live by the notion of "united we stand, divided we fall" or that of "divide and conquer." It's nearly impossible to get on one accord if our value system is as far off as it is now.

Please don't confuse my words here. I believe

that everyone can be a leader in one or more areas, but it is important to be a contributor to the general Black community at all times. There must be a balance between the two. Being a Black male empowerment group leader should not stop you from connecting with the rest of the general Black body at your university. We are intersectional people. We hold many different identities. It's important to acknowledge your identities while never forgetting to organize around our most significant commonality, *our skin color*. It's our gender, background, culture, and interests that make us unique.

There isn't one single way to be Black. We must understand this and accept our differences while understanding how we're viewed by people who aren't Black. We see the differences amongst ourselves, but others don't. These differences have been used to divide us, without us even knowing. This is why it's important not to get caught up in digging too deep into narrowing down your identity. Those who capitalize on our dysfunction are counting on you to separate yourself from other Black people.

The needs, wants, demands, and desires of Black organizations should mirror those across all college campuses. Some Black organizations adhere to certain guidelines (e.g., college major, graduating year, etc.). This is fine. The majority of Black organizations want the best for Black students, but they have a distorted idea of how to get there. That said, students often join organizations that don't benefit the masses of Black students. Just because an organization is deemed as a prestigious Black organization doesn't mean it's useful or sufficient for Black students as a whole. One evaluation question to ask in regards to these concerns is *who does this organization help besides its relatively small group of members?*

Khalil Masi hit the nail on the head when he said, "Black students have been injected with a belief system that undermines Black collective progress in this country. They are told that their desires will be met if they follow the prescription that whites prescribed, such as: doing well in school, joining the student government, speaking a certain way, and investing money in the system with hopes of a return. If the prescription is followed, the Black student will change. They will identify themselves and other Blacks by how disciplined they are to these beliefs. When the Black student gets around his or her educated friends, they will realize that their friends don't practice what they do...and they will disassociate from them. The argument as to why they cannot hang with them isn't because they are poor and vice versa. Likely, the college student is poorer than the non-college student. The student believes his old friends are not successful because they aren't woke enough.

They're ignorant of the right beliefs."

The Black college student typically fails to connect the struggles that they face as a college student to the struggles of the non-college student, which creates a disconnect and separation that hurts both people. This is a classic example of divide and conquer. We've been brainwashed into thinking that becoming a successful college student involves some form of an imaginary checklist. This deprives Black students of our greatest gift...our creativity. It narrows down the definition of success, which caters to the belief that Black students have to be viewed as successful by our peers. In a perfect world, the Black artist on your campus—who's created great work and has been recognized by the university and his or her peers—should receive the same love and respect as the Divine Nine members on your campus. In most instances, this is not the case. Once again, our value system is off.

Respected members of organizations play an enormous role in Black excellence. Still, it is dangerous to view any group of people as the top level of success for Black college students. There is no one single way to be Black. Therefore, one single achievement shouldn't be used as a measuring stick of how successful or respectable an individual is. Blacks have faith in a system they've created within a broken system on and off campus, rooted in individualism, arrogance, materialism, faith, and intellectual laziness. Who benefits from our individualism?

We've created this illusion of a hierarchy within the Black college community that hinders everyone. Our approach should be more horizontal than it is vertical. The vertical path is what we have in place now. There's an unfortunate willingness to undercut each other to get to the top for a certain level of prestige. To reach the top, we'll create organizations under the motive of false recognition to build up our name and influence. We are willing to do all these things when, in reality, we don't have to. We can operate on a level playing field. We can all gain a certain level of respect and love from our peers that still allows us all to have a part in doing the work of Black progression. **Dissatisfaction breeds improvement, while satisfaction inhibits complacency.**

As the old saying goes, heavy is the head that wears the crown. If you are willing to wear the crown of Black excellence, then you must also be ready and humble enough to carry the burdens of solving Black issues.

How Can We Fix It?

We've made it to the end of the book! We know what the problems are...and I believe I have a solution to shift our perspective from individualism to a unified front. Because you've read *A Message to Black College Students* in its entirety, it's safe to say that you understand the shift I'm referring to. My solution may not be the ideal solution for your community or personal situation; nevertheless, take what I say into consideration, and utilize your own knowledge to make the change you want to see happen.

I've categorized Black college students as creative in their way of thinking. But now is the time to use that creativity in ways that push us—the Black community—forward. We can do this by shifting into solution-based thinking:

We figure out what we truly stand for.
We focus on the root cause of our issues

instead of the symptoms.

We pay attention to our miseducation, lack of unity, food sovereignty, and distorted view(s) of success.

We organize like never before.

We strategize based on our personal skill sets for the uplifting of all Black people.

We study the times and circumstances of the past and use it as fuel for the future.

We create opportunities for each other because we know that no one else will.

We remain true to who we are, regardless of what the outside tells us we need to be.

Acknowledgments

B.F Nukrumah- 6 A's of Manhood for African American Men
Sherrie- My Hope Village Detroit
Raphael Wright-Make the Hood Great Again
Kyle McCurty-Henry Goes to an HBCU
Aaliyah Gross
Khalil Masi
Andre Ellington-Editor
Alona Turner-Cover Art
Nailah Harvey-Editor
Jamel Fortune
E'Lexus Daniels
Joelle Sanders
(Anyone else who gave me feedback/guidance as I wrote this book)

CPSIA information can be obtained
at www.ICGtesting.com
Printed in the USA
LVHW101500020921
696791LV00015B/879/J

9 780996 094382